THE BOOK

Universal Kingdom Print
Page-Turners
& Upcoming Author Works
www.universalkingdominternational.com

The Book
By, **Anjeza Angie Gega**

The Creation of a Manifesto, Book 1:
Black & Blue
By, **Cheryl Dorsey**

The Project: Limitless Series, Book 1:
The Success Initiative
By, **R.J. Tolson**

The Twinacity Series, Book 1:
Twinacity
By, **Ashley Mills**

For previews of upcoming works
by Anjeza Angie Gega, and more
information about the author, visit:
www.angiegega.com

THE BOOK

Anjeza Angie Gega

This edition first published in 2014
© 2014 Anjeza Angie Gega

RJTIO/Universal Kingdom Print
Published by Unviersal Kingdom Print
United States of America
10 9 8 7 6 5 4 3 2 1

For details on our global editorial offices, customers
service, and information about applying for permission
to reuse the copyright material in this book, see our
website www.universalkingdominternational.com

Many Universal Kingdom Print books are available at
special quantity discounts for bulk purchase. For details,
contact the author, author's official representative, or
publisher.

Editor and Designer: Nathan Elsey

ISBN-13: 978-0990329916
ISBN: 0990329917
Universal Kingdom Print

The definition of

POTION:

A liquid with healing,
magical,

or poisonous properties.
"A love potion"

My quotes aim to heal
while staying on people's
mind as a fragrance. Magic
potion formula created in
the lab of life...

CAUTION!!!Ingredients
include: Love, Pain,
Strength, Lessons,
Enlightenment, Hope,
Forgiveness, and Faith...
Mix them responsively!!!

POTION #1

"Find yourself in the peace of faith, the choice of trust... and the assurance that the true LOVE of Creator wraps you up every day with the masterpiece of his work."

POTION #2

"The worst judgment is the one we give to ourselves... The deepest pain is the Guilt we dress our conscience with... The most successful work have been fruits of an unexplainable faith in oneself. No matter who, what, how, when, and where... at the end of the day... It's You lifting up You... or You sinking You... You have a choice! Make it! You have a question! Answer it!"

POTION #3

"Rain to wash your pain away... Wind that wakes up your soul and says hey... Sun that inspires your thoughts... It's a half full cup... It's your choice... Unending blue skies that bring hope of a never dying feeling... Love will fly to you... Believe it... Dark nights have a quick expiration date... Rainbow's beauty makes one forget the rain..."

POTION #4

"Don't struggle to create
the perfect gold cage for
the bird... when all he
wants to do is fly away...
Don't chase to catch
butterflies and collect
them in a glass box...
when their beauty stands
in them flapping their
wings and sitting on your
nose... Don't try too hard
to impress... Love is
born... raised... and
lasts forever without you
even knowing. Don't
calculate... Just smile,
and be yourself..."

POTION #5

"Don't get opinions from
the world...

Get answers from The
Lord..."

THE BOOK

POTION #6

"In happiness, I can have
the world... In sadness, I
will have the real
souls...
This is the true quantity-
quality law."

POTION #7

"I always seek to satisfy
my heart... This would
have been so selfish of me
if you didn't know the
truth... my heart beats to
heal...each one of you."

POTION #8

"Silence is a good
answer... but not everyone
deserves it."

THE BOOK

POTION #9

"I don't get along with
the sane... They have no
sense of risk, dreams, or
faith... They look at life
as if they were in the
elementary grade... They
read but they don't
understand... They hear
but still complain... They
calculate... Their life is
an inherited path, not...
watch me... I'll change my
fate... They lack
colors... They lack sun...
They sit and dine on a
place called 'Judge' ..."

POTION #10

"The biggest gift of life
is passion... Water it...
It can dry from the heat
of opinions..."

POTION #11

"Little people complain.
Big people do. Little
minds argue. Big ones
move. Tiny hearts can't
see... beyond themselves.
Big ones are slowly...
changing the game."

POTION #12

"I don't have many enemies because
I have only few friends."

POTION #13

"I don't forget how the
past treated me... because
it made me someone, I am
happy with. I don't regret
how I treated my past...
because I was always
honest and lead by my
heart..."

POTION #14

"The most dangerous
feeling is the one that
has no cause. You don't
know how to fix it... The
most powerful voice is the
silent one. You don't know
how to stop it."

POTION #15

"Independence feels so
right. My choices. My
mistakes. My achievements.
My fails. My yes. My no.
My world... Some close.
Some far. Some in. Some
out... Some good... Some
bad... Some left. Some
came back... My mind. My
heart. My soul. They
scream so loud. I stop.
I'm worth a sunny day... a
love that never ends... a
smile that never dies... a
hug that speaks no lies...
The truth touches my mind.
I'm sorry for letting you
down. I swear to you
today... No lies. No pain.
No lies."

POTION #16

"A rushed Yes... means a
quick No... Reflect...
Words should not be loud
to impress... World will
clap for your shallow
success... but a noble
heart won't be ok... if
the roots of your words
land on cement."

THE BOOK

POTION #17

"Wisdom is a power candy
wrapped in pain..."

POTION #18

"I feel bad for every
being that looks outside
of itself for an approval.
I'd rather be crazy for
daring than insecure for
caring."

POTION #19

"Dance under the beat of
your own drum. The best
music is the one you
create and the world
doesn't understand."

POTION #20

"Money is like a gun.
Depends on the person that
owns it."

POTION #21

"I refuse to color love
with any other color but
red... I refuse to add
pre-positions or ending it
with dramatic metaphors of
rain... Getting old and
dying... No, that is not
true... I want to always
remember love... as red,
young, and never blue...
Because when it touches
you, it changes your
life... even your breath
has a different sound...
So just keep it at that...
sweet heart of mine. Some
are temporary, other last
your whole life... They
are all beautiful...
Remember that... and just
smile... "

POTION #22

"I used to smile to hide
the pain. Now I smile
because I forgot how to go
back."

POTION #23

"Success ends when your
happiness becomes a duty,
your choices become
confined from society's
definitions of what's
right, and what you do...
is just a show for some
fake applauses that
temporary iron the
wrinkles of your life..."

POTION #24

"Sometimes we channel
success as a slap on the
face of the one that never
believed in us... But we
got it all wrong... That
impure energy used to take
us high, won't ever
deliver to any peace of
mind."

THE BOOK

POTION #25

"Confidence is what covers
your heart after reality
undresses your life..."

POTION #26

"You are a pack of
rainbows waiting to light
hope on somebody's rain...
Keep loving beyond your
'doesn't make sense'...
No, it doesn't make sense
at all... But it will make
a good song..."

POTION #27

"In a tangible world I
see, I crave to close my
eyes and fall in love with
the unknown, the
untouchable, the
everlasting... "

POTION #28

"I always saw in people
not what they were today,
but what they could be
tomorrow. And that way of
thinking···justified deep
care and forgiveness..."

POTION #29

"I asked for a voice to
speak···You gave me notes
to breath... I asked for a
difference to make... You
gave life to my feet and
said dance... I have no
hands to heal... but I
have a voice that sings...
I have no millions in the
bank... but a heart that
plans philanthropy one
day... This is who I am...
good or bad... right or
wrong... Your plan brought
me here... It's no fail...
You are perfect... You
make no mistakes..."

POTION #30

"You don't always live
ugly because you deserve
it... bigger plans got you
in training... to
understand low... so you
can appreciate high... to
overcome darkness... so
you can seek light..."

POTION #31

"Every person that walks
in your life is a door
that leads to a spiritual
growth, never a setback.
Seeing it, is up to you.
Allowing it to affect in
any other way, is where
you fail..."

POTION #32

"Strong is the only thing
I know.. and yes maybe
sometimes I want to
crawl.. cry on the
shoulders of someone that
knows... someone that
doesn't judge my
fall... but right now ...
right now is time to press
on"

POTION #33

"I am in love with someone
I have never met... Is
God's angel waiting for
his turn to walk on my
path... Until then, I will
smile and live... because
actions are healing for
the one in need..."

POTION #34

"Woman, is your God's
given right to be
respected... And if
somehow they don't, You
should demand it... You
set the record straight...
You show them how is
done... Don't settle to
get by... You are uniquely
blessed... Demand the
best! Train the world...
You will receive, what you
allow them to give..."

POTION #35

"Love of a good woman
makes a man attractive...

Love of a good man makes a
woman blessed."

POTION #36

"Have you ever thought where you would be without those No-s in the past... those closed doors, those rejections... that guy/girl you liked so much but it didn't work out, that job that you thought was the answer but then you got offered something better? The destiny... The written... The journey... The destination... And there is so much more... Just smile at every closed door... Sometimes they lead not into a magical garden... but just a wall that is rotten... REGRET NOT!!! GOD is in Control. And he wants a magical future for you. Rest assured!!!"

POTION #37

"A partner is a reflection
you see in your self-
worth. If your choices are
constantly leading you to
someone wrong. You need to
STOP... and find yourself
first. "

POTION #38

"I have chosen to see my
spiritual scars as self
drawn tattoos that express
the birth of a warrior."

POTION #39

"TRUE LOVE is LIKE GOD...

IT never hurts. .."

POTION #40

"True success comes with the maturity of knowing priorities."

POTION #41

"If today you feel like
nobody... look up and
change your mind... you
were created by a
miraculous God... It is
often His pleasure to make
something amazing out of
nothing... Trust⋯ Your
time is coming."

POTION #42

"Don't be the reader of
somebody's glory... Be the
protagonist of your own
bestselling story."

POTION #43

"The world is visually
oriented. Catch them with
your look, maintain them
with your heart, lock them
with your mind."

POTION #44

"Self-worth leads to
achievements that turn you
into an expensive brand...

affordable only by a rich
soul."

POTION #45

"I don't want to pray for
a pair of shorts... when
God has prepared a whole
wardrobe. I want HIS
plan... not mine···because
fear asks for less but
faith delivers more··· what
seems impossible to me...
He can deliver in
1. 2. 3... "

POTION #46

"Faith is a crazy trait. We see things that are not there. Fall in love with what we can't explain... Draw a future based on a wind... Seek for thrills that earth hasn't seen... During all this we don't understand... that being crazy is not a sickness... just a difference... and a dare... from which the world is scared... If "crazy" takes over this world... Dare... Do it... Change it... Reach it... Unlimited... Chance... Would be the strongest leaders... up to date!"

POTION #47

"You act like Heaven hates
you when you get that
NO... Spoiled brat you
are... What if that just
saved your life...
preparing you for a bigger
YES to come. Have some
faith... You unfaithful
one!!!"

POTION #48

"Walk away from
expectations of the
world... and build a
life... listening to your
soul... Pack wings for
that heart of yours...
spark angel's dust
wherever you go..."

POTION #49

"Get lost in the fantasy
that excites your spirit,
not just your body... Find
the eternal spark that
charges your purpose...
not just your chemistry."

POTION #50

"I don't have time to
judge... I desire to Love.
I don't wish to gossip...
but rather just focus...
because the ones that
talk, don't do... and the
ones that do, have no time
to talk... Live, Love, and
Laugh!!! This life is a
business climb... What's
the profit in your waste
of time?"

POTION #51

"Success with no love···is
misery in command...
Achievement with no
passion... is an empty
house caving in."

POTION #52

"Life won't give you the
commodity to cry on your
own tempo. Don't linger
long over there... Pick up
the pieces... Put them
together... Create a
song... and dance. I have
zero tolerance for waste
of time. I am constantly
growing and seeking to
refine... so when life
steps on my toes... a
reflective behavior of
protection... screams to
her face. Don't join my
party... without being
invited!"

POTION #53

"You control nothing...
All can be taken in a
split second... So tell
me... What's the fuzz and
buzz about you stepping up
your game... buying cars
and mansions... visiting
Paris and London···? How
about food for
thoughts...? BUILD YOUR
HEART AND SOUL, not bank
accounts and walls..."

POTION #54

"The world judges your
actions...

while God searches your
heart..."

POTION #55

"Some people succeed.
Other applaud. Your
destiny was written. Which
one is your call?"

POTION #56

"Stars will align...

Miracles will happen...

Golden doors will open...

Angels will cross your
path...

Will you be ready for all
that?"

POTION #57

"LOVE has a price... It's
called TIME... Give it to
that special one. Build
memories that will never
die. There is nothing more
precious than time... and
if you got it not... then
you don't love..."

POTION #58

"Pay attention to the
voice of your red fat
pretty cute heart... And
don't be afraid... God
doesn't place dreams there
by mistake. Learn to love
freely, loudly,
enormously,
unconditionally... The
rest is not in your
hands... Don' t be
afraid... A long time of
you trying and wishing...
can be fulfilled in five
minutes, when God takes
over, your whole being..."

POTION #59

"It's not about distance
and awards... It's about
growth and love. Further
doesn't mean
deeper···Alright? Take your
time... Make it right...
Easy comes, easy goes...
This life is yours... not
just a show... All I want
is to be happy... and the
definition of that is not
in the dictionary. Love...
Think... Do... On Re-
loop!!! Live, Love, Let it
Be... This is Me!!!"

POTION #60

"And to the one with whom
you don't puzzle click…
you'll find the strength
to say… I am sure there
is a perfect one for you…
That just... ain't me, I
guess. Don't drag
yourself in the mud… You
won't come out of it...
dressed in white…"

POTION #61

"All you need to be
successful is a dish of
passion, a glass of
determination, a spoon of
talent, herbs of I am
crazy enough to dive into
this all... laying on a
table of character...
covered by a cloth of
faith..."

POTION #62

"What you leave... It will
leave you... Time moves
fast... World changes...
The need to cope with
presence and absence...
leads to the birth of a
new initiative... Letting
go of the old and
embracing the new... There
is no such thing as
waiting infinite... So
don't let go of what you
love... or get ruled by
that thought called
pride... Wondering can
build false conclusions...
Misunderstanding is the
offspring of delusion...
You love? Show it! You
miss? Say it! You hurt?
Express it! You don't like
it? Scream it!!!"

POTION #63

"You need to act as a
grown up in this monster
game. Curved lips and
teeth... it is sure taken
as weak... So keep your
sugar for who deserves
it.. and grab the mindful
weapons for the
apocalypses..."

POTION #64

"I never questioned a
closed door or losing
someone... because my life
is under heavenly
control... The temporaries
don't matter... the
permanent will be a
JACKPOT win served on a
silver platter..."

POTION #65

"Don't get in God's way by
messing up with His
plan... Yourself. Your
presence on earth is
temporary... Embrace
that... Live that... Don't
ruin it with your choices
of sadness and self
destruction actions. You
are beautiful... You are
special... You are
masterly created for a
greater purpose."

POTION #66

"I love deeply... Give
fully... Sacrifice
completely... Hurt
easily... Hit the floor
loudly... Heal swiftly...
Stand up quickly..."

POTION #67

"Pain lasts longer
sometimes... not because
of its size... but because
of the choice to let it
affect us longer..."

POTION #68

"The biggest gift you can

give someone is the

never dying flower of
faith...

held by the stem of
Hope...

born by the roots of
Love..."

POTION #69

"It's not about being
right... It's about being
happy... It's not about
calculated results... It's
about chances... Jump with
no regret... Feel the air
touch your face... Search
your wings... It gets
tiring to walk on your
feet."

POTION #70

"To love someone...

means to forgive their
past and

believe in their future."

POTION #71

"If you are not capable to
love, don't hurt... "

POTION #72

"I still crave to wake up
to a wonderful moment,
beautiful text, a great
email, an amazing dream
opportunity... so it can
prove and re-prove my
belief... that spirits
meet while you dream...
that life arranges itself
like a movie... while your
body charges for the next
adventure..."

POTION #73

"Be happy... You owe it to
your heart...
Be wise... You owe it to
your life..."

POTION #74

"If you are married to
perfection, you will never
be free!!! Grow and
constantly upgrade... but
don't suffocate yourself
with what isn' t there···.
Let your heart, thoughts,
and desires fly... so they
can complete somebody' s
else life.... Sometimes
all the world needs is a
piece of you... undressed,
makeup free... Just the
way YOU are···

So, just BE···"

POTION #75

"Break the walls that
confine your freedom...
Destroy the reputation
that suffocates your
passion"

THE BOOK

POTION #76

"Love has the ability to
iron the
wrinkles of worries..."

POTION #77

"I rather hug my torn
pillows in peace...

than lay on sinful gold
sheets..."

POTION #78

"For every worldly unseen
effort... There is a
heavenly "thank you"
letter... For every
worldly unanswered
request... There is a
heavenly given
response..."

POTION #79

"Let your mind seek
paradise... Let your soul
touch no mud... Let your
hand stretch into a
mistake... so it will
learn to not repeat
again... Let the world
speak and shout... God's
opinion is all that
counts..."

THE BOOK

POTION #80

"When you know HEAVEN,
Earth's pain has no power
on You!..."

POTION #81

"I have lit a candle in
that beautiful lonely
heart of yours... knock,
knock... Anybody there?...
I have lost my way in the
forest of life... met so
many beasts... but I found
hope tonight... Can I come
in? Can you cook me some
thoughts?... Or maybe lets
take this slow... hot tea
would be ok... next to
your heart's turned off
fireplace... Keep me
warm... introduce me to
your eyes... I want to see
the water fall... and then
let's dance slow. Let your
body speak... Let my heart
touch yours... Now you are
not alone... "

POTION #82

"When a one way road leads
to the wall... make an
illegal U-turn..."

POTION #83

"World will dress you with
guilt and mud... or strip
you down to fear and
doubts... Understand the
facts... Know the truth...
Change the fashion... Put
on your favorite outfit,
made by: Confidence!!!"

POTION #84

"People like to say...

'Where was God when I was
hurt?'

I like to tell them...

Where were you... when God
said 'Don't'..."

POTION #85

"I won't worry if my
today's happiness will be
extended tomorrow...
because I don't want to
miss out on that butterfly
feeling in my stomach..."

POTION #86

"Don't worry if the
language of your giving
gets lost in
translation... Don't cease
being light... even when
darkness temporary blurs
the sight... Rest sure...
You will always impact
someone's life... Their
heart will listen... Their
mind will think... Their
soul will question... even
when their body won't
always be ready for the
action..."

POTION #87

"Time is the highest level
of unshaped wealth... The
wise invest it only on
matters that profit
happiness..."

POTION #88

"Let's just be serious
over here... and act
crazy... Gratitude with a
dose of happiness... Let's
break rules, but hurt
nobody... Taking chances
with no parachute... But
practicing landing way too
good... Stupid actions,
behind a smart plan...
Live it up... It's your
life!!!"

POTION #89

"If you happen to steal
the guy from another...
just know... is not
because you are pretty and
irresistible... It just
means... he is a disloyal
cheater... Women take
pride of breaking up
someone from his girl or
wife... They don't really
understand... Their action
just won them copper and
iron, not gold and
diamond..."

POTION #90

"I rather have lunch with
a mute person, the eyes of
whom speak a library, than
someone with flattering
propositions, which he
doesn't even know the
meaning."

POTION #91

"Every action has a past
and a future. Don't be so
quick to judge the
present. There is a reason
why you are acting this
way today... forgive
yourself... There is a
place where your actions
will take you tomorrow...
Choose the best."

POTION #92

"A good woman doesn't need
to play games... Her
character speaks for
itself... Stand solid...
The estimator you want···
knows the value of a
precious stone."

POTION #93

"World's opinion about
your future doesn't matter
if they are doing nothing
for you to reach it...
World's judgment about
your present doesn't
matter if they didn't walk
on your past high heels...
Don't wait for approval...
You got the light inside
you... Don't bow in front
of judgment... There is
only one God you bow to...
Don't take NO for an
answer... to whatever God
turned into a YES... and
is perfect."

POTION #94

"The stars are so
beautiful tonight! I just
want to sit and have a
talk with them. Ask them
how come they are so
pretty, quiet, and
humble... and why humans
are so small, egotistic,
and just mumble... I just
want to talk to my stars
tonight... and promise to
wear them one day on
stage... and when they ask
me... where did I get that
beautiful dress... I can
just say... Special Order,
God made it Himself..."

POTION #95

"I don't walk backwards in
life... I'll give you my
all... If you are too
blind to see... It is your
fault... I'll be your
blessing or lesson... Call
it what you want... But I
will never eat... what has
been thrown on the
floor... I am a human...
not a dog..."

POTION #96

"Be strong enough to give
with no fear... Be selfish
enough to pull out with no
scars..."

POTION #97

"In an ocean filled with creatures... If Nemo doesn't find you... Don't forget to give a chance to Flipper..."

POTION #98

"World keeps breeding
clones that fit in a mummy
casket... while I refuse
to pretend I am a
mannequin that just
satisfies the eyes of the
strangers..."

POTION #99

"Don't try to be someone
you are not... so you
don't attract someone that
you don't want..."

POTION #100

"While climbing the ladder
to tangible success...
many forget their heart on
the first step..."

POTION #101

"Shallow vs. Deep,

I tried taking that first
pill...

But my system was allergic
to it..."

POTION #102

"What do I do with the
truth? Swallow it? But
that's not fair... Truth
was made to be free··· and
so I dare...Lies I destroy
or bring them to light...
I'm becoming someone that
loves truth more than
prices and piedestal"

POTION #103

"Waste of time is
expensive...

I am not rich enough to
afford it..."

POTION #104

"The world needs to get a
membership in confidence
and love... not gyms and
country clubs..."

POTION #105

"Scientists can't accept
God because they don't
have a formula that
explains faith and true
love..."

POTION #106

"Nobody taught me life...
I just have always been so
stubborn to give up on
what I love!!!"

POTION #107

"Seeds of distraction
can't build roots

in a grateful heart."

POTION #108

"Women get a bruised
confidence after a
relationship fails... Here
is an instant herbal
medicine... Next time...
Get a hobby, not a blind
thief..."

POTION #109

"If you have given
expecting something in
return... then you haven't
given at all... Scratch
that self-titled award···Do
it right, or not all···"

POTION #110

"Confidence is nothing
more than an attitude that
doesn't care about
rejection. You have seen
the No-s..hit the closed
doors, been stepped on by
shiny shoes··· that have
painful stories to tell if
they only had a voice to
confess···YET..through all
this···You continue···You
reach···You believe··· and
with a smile on your face
you think··· The YES is
coming···today. tomorrow,
soon··· Dust sits on your
face from the trials of
life···you wipe it off with
an innocent
smile···character
tight..you stand up···"

POTION #111

"The woman waits for the
right man...

the man waits for the
right time..."

POTION #112

"Feelings are like
hunger... If you don't
feed them with actions...
They will starve and cease
existing."

POTION #113

"Here is my philosophy in
life... It doesn't hurt to
try... You ask, you
knock... And if you get a
no... That is already what
you had ...so no harm at
all... But by doing and
trying... A miracle might
be met .. And then the yes
can be a blessing for you
and the rest. I was asked
one day... How do I deal
with rejection in what I
do... I said: honestly I
don't think about it. I
plant the seed and give it
my all... And then move on
to a different soil... If
it blooms then it was
meant to be and if it
doesn't ... There are more
soils for me. "

POTION #114

"Don't dance in devil's
party and think you will
leave from there with both
feet!"

POTION #115

"There is always "Not Yet"
excuse to life... waiting
for 'the right moment' –
they justify⋯ If being a
mermaid is what you love
to do... Stop starring at
the water⋯ and learn how
to swim. "

POTION #116

"Darkness will linger. Bad
choices will taste better.
Pain will surface. Where
did you go wrong? Cuz you
know... somehow, you chose
that all along!!"

POTION #117

"In a world where
perfection is needed to
reach that next big
thing... the sunlight
comes as a reminder of
God's smile and promise
that says... Pressure
off... You don't need to
win my love... I have
gifted it to you before I
placed you in your
mother's womb."

POTION #118

"Seven times down, eight
times up.

Life is a battlefield...

WISDOM is your sight.

ABILITY is your shield...

CHARACTER is your sword.

Now go win the war!!!"

POTION #119

"When the world kicks your
confidence to the
ground... Don't get comfy
with the dust... Stand up.
Head high... You are a
human, not a reptile..."

POTION #120

"Reward yourself every day
with something or someone
that makes your heart
move."

POTION #121

"A star is a rock lit by
the sun...

Remember that, when you
think you reached the
skies... It's not about
the value you have...
It's about the blessing,
grace, and light someone
else decided to shed. A
sweet tongue can brake
bones...

A kind word can heal
wounds.

Be humble! Serve to
others!"

POTION #122

"Be a filter in life...

there is a lot to ignore...

Be a sponge in life...

There is a lot to learn...

When you understand the
meaning of these words...

you'll find a gem...

that will make you rich. "

POTION #123

"Don't be the jackpot
winner of an undeserving
player... be the gift to
an equal soul... that when
he looks in the mirror of
your heart... he sees the
missing puzzle of his
life."

POTION #124

"I - (deduct) waste of
time...

x (multiplied) by the
perfect love You give

/ (divided) by the choices
I take...

+ (add) the passion
attached to my actions =
(equals)

···My formula to
success..."

POTION #125

"Don't be the hero of
misery... Be the changer
of destiny... What were
the odds for me to be
where I am... Minus
million... I would
guess... But life is not
defined by potential while
you sit on the couch... is
built by passions while
you dig for treasure the
underground... You got
looks...? So got everyone
else... You can't compete
with the perfection in the
"surgery LA" ... You got
talent...? So got everyone
else... but the question
is what do you do with all
that?... You got
passion... work...
persistence...? Now,
That's your niche. Stick
to it!!!"

POTION #126

"You seek love outside of
your body and embrace
every comparison they give
you to an established
figure... You smile at the
idea of being a clone.
Why? Why are you afraid to
embrace and love
yourself... Stop
memorizing the steps of
success someone else
made... There is only one
formula to happiness...
It's called

H. E. ART !!! Listen...
Follow···Fall together, and
then again try... Be a new
Rosa Park, Martin Luther
King, or Joan D' Arc."

POTION #127

"Learn to be attached
not... because there is
nothing you own... Be
afraid not... Yesterday
was a lesson... Tomorrow
is unknown... Today is
trying to talk... can you
hear what she says? Stand
up and dance... don't
forget the chance... the
race... the face... the
love... the breath... the
pain... the thought... the
tears you shed... No
limitations to your
reach.. The world said
it... I heard... but they
are afraid... they don't
know... The light... the
miracle... the voice, the
dream. .. LIVE!!!...
Breath IN... Gratitude and
LOVE... Breath OUT
Forgiveness... and Giving
UP!!!"

POTION #128

"I don't believe in
luck... I believe in
blessings.

I don't rely on MAYBE-s…
I work only for YES-es."

POTION #129

"When you start
something.... start it
fully, deeply,
passionately... with the
all or nothing thought in
mind... When you leave
something... leave it
empty, surely,
completely... with no
crumbs or doubts... that
can invite you back when
you get hungry."

POTION #130

"We have

THE POWER

to tell ourselves what to
do, and

THE CHOICE

to believe that it will be
delivered."

POTION #131

"The flowers, the words...
the travel... romance...
kisses and promises... The
one you dreamed of... It
will all come one day...
Wait... Don't lose
faith... Learn to not rush
the baking of the cake...
Your age... Your family...
The World... You got
nothing to prove to
anyone. Wait!!! It's often
red in the matters of
heart... But when you see
that green... You will
speed to the max...
Freeway's empty... Cops
are sleeping... Just you
and him spinning cars and
winning... Adrenaline
high... Adventures

escalate... You look at
each other...

-Silence-

What's going on? Out of
breath you both say:

'This is it··· I guess!!!.

-Laughs-

POTION #132

"The world has no ceiling,

the dreams have no

limits... "

POTION #133

"It's the nature's law...
No pity in love... So
instead of begging for
attention of someone··· and
suffering that you are not
good enough... Work on
growing and becoming
complete...a better
individual and partner,
think career advancement,
strengthen your heart and
character... So when your
eyes meet that one of a
kind... you won't be
worried to hide the
skeletons of your life.
But just one look... two
steps... an invitation to
slow dance... a smile...
some laughs... And who
knows ···what else
potentially will come...
of two souls that were the
best... and found each
other... that one day..."

POTION #134

"A good word towards your
worries won't fix
anything...

A bad word towards your
dreams won't change
destiny...

It's up to you... to build
or destroy...

The talk in the background
is just a noise."

POTION #135

"Tell me what you know...
Not what I fear...
Lord, Your confidence and
wisdom... is the air I
need."

POTION #136

"A person who doesn't take
advantage of the need and
the weakness of the other
gender, is a noble one...
I see the contrary all the
time... It's all about the
physical approach that
leads to a temporary
satisfaction... Narrow
minded... They all speak
the same language... Makes
me wonder...

Are they all so
illiterate?···"

POTION #137

"Don't cry. Fix it..."

POTION #138

"You can't buy freedom...
You can't buy happiness...
You can't buy love... You
can't buy blessings... You
can't buy God... You can't
buy heaven... Heard you
were confused, talking
about deeds... scared of
expiration date, gasping
for the calculator,
winning points to fix your
credits... Take a deep
breath... Kneel, pray, and
wait··· wait for grace...
It is gifted... not
bought... Given... not
earned."

POTION #139

"If the heart doesn't
speak... The mind should
not mime...

A mute musical is pathetic
and waste of life..."

POTION #140

"They say things are not
easy... Relationships are
work... I say... Forget
about it all... What God
has prepared for you won't
ever scratch... but
embrace... embrace you to
a different level... You
will ask him... were you
by any chance born in
heaven...? I am all or
nothing kind of
creature... I don't have a
problem to ride alone...
But if destiny is
preparing my angel... I
just ask one more wish...
Please pack him with
wings... I don't care
about his car or boat... I
just want to fly with him
to another world... "

POTION #141

"If having faith makes one
crazy because is not based
on visual facts... then my
dreams can definitely
define my status of
thinking... as totally
insane."

POTION #142

"Status without heart is
like a chair with rotten
feet... Heart without
status is like stairway
ready to be built..."

POTION #143

"Commit to your
passions...
Distractions are
temporary."

POTION #144

"When heart acts... there
is no mind to stop it...
When heart gives... there
is nothing to regret of
it... When heart speaks...
just follow it... At night
I am glad for at least one
thing... I put my head on
the pillow in a perfect
peace... because I know
that intentionally... I
haven't hurt a living
thing... "

POTION #145

"I have chosen the
unordinary...

to tell ignorance...
Really?"

POTION #146

"When it rains... dance
under those angels'
tears... When the strong
wind blows... fly on
miracles... When the world
shoots you with words...
collect those bullets and
write a song... When
reality seems to be
cruel... take a second...
look inside you... have a
meeting with your heart
and mind... somehow... a
wrong turn was done...
Don't blame anyone for
where you are... There is
no time to criticize...
Collect all you have...
and **SHINE!!!**"

POTION #147

"If I was asked to write a
one sentence bio of my
life... I would say:
'ME, is just a collection
of many YOU's'... Past,
present, future, and
forever... In order to
help, one needs to
identify... In order to
identify, one needs to
understand... a journey...
self discovery... mirrored
in your glossy eyes...
filled with passion and
desire... to just
Breath... and then Live...
to just Love... and
hopefully Laugh... to just
Do, and finally Be...
Me... You... "

POTION #148

"I am not always strong...
I just make myself always
busy... So when weakness
knocks on the door
reminding me how one
'thing' walked away... I
remind weakness that I am
busy with 100 other things
that care."

POTION #149

"May the waterfall of your
grace shower my thoughts
and saturate my thirst for
truth and true love... I
belong to you... There is
no doubt... So let me
remind myself and the
world just one thing... No
weapon built against your
kind··· will ever prosper
in this lifetime..."

POTION #150

"I won't ever be the one
to send you to nursing
home... or tell you that I
am busy and hang up the
phone... Because I
remember when I was little
and weak... I remember how
much I received... so I
won't ever be the one that
forgets to give...

Mother. Love. Gratitude"

POTION #151

"Lead me to the waters You
know...
And I'll swim the way You
taught."

POTION #152

"The second handed
abilities that I paid
little attention... are
now roaring opening the
doors to my first
options... Never doubt the
molding God's plan
holds... If it's in your
path... embrace it... no
need to dissect it... or
time measure it... just
take it... When God is in
your life... nothing in
your path will make you
drown... maybe just sink
you deep... and teach you
faith, the necessary
weapon for this life's
video game···"

POTION #153

"There are two factors
that influence success:

GENES and CHOICES

One chooses you. . The other
you do···!

Calculate the mate you
wed···so you won' t be
hunted by your
offspring' s nightmares. "

POTION #154

"When they close one door
in your face... and you
stand in front of it with
faith... another brighter
one opens up... that has
the power to make you
smile..."

POTION #155

"I am a perfectionist that
seeks no perfection, but
satisfaction. Because
perfection becomes
boring...but satisfaction
becomes inspiring..."

POTION #156

"In silence I touch my
soul... It feels so
soft... Powerful as an
energetic source that
makes the empty cave
work... and the body that
looks like the inner part
of a watch... The
mechanical movement
demands oil to flow... a
heavenly ointment that in
the darkness can make
anything glow...Heart and
mind... army positioned...
They listen.. Wait for HIS
command... Taking the
truth and making it the
wish of youth... Obedience
to the max... Sometimes...
Then others I fail... I am
ashamed... But HE
assures... Don't stress...
I love you beyond all your
guilts and fails."

POTION #157

"Here is a great medicine
to all your worries...
Stay Busy!!! The multiple
doors of productivity and
self discover abilities...
will gift you a positive
futuristic inspiration
that makes the past such a
nonsense... Fall in love
with your soul... It will
never let you down..."

POTION #158

"I don't understand the games some women conduct to get the taken man... Is like a challenge computer game for them... They get so focused to impress... they plot so they can conquer the plan... Why would you waste time on the used one... split his attention... feed of the leftover crumbs, or sink in the darkness of lust...? I have one simple rule... If his eyes, heart, and hands belong to another... then he is just simply gone from my radar. I don't even think anymore or look in his eyes... He made his choice... and here is mine!"

POTION #159

"Desperation leads to
failure... Cockiness leads
to loneliness... So keep
it real... and you will
succeed... and if you
don't... at least you
didn't have to struggle...
remembering the lying
script."

POTION #160

"A new step today is
better than none
yesterday. No matter how
much you hurt... Earn...
or learn... You will
always be a winner in the
spiritual terms."

POTION #161

"There is no formula for
this life... just like a
new mom... The instincts
are born for you to
survive. So quit studying
somebody else's life. We
are all different elements
in the chemistry chart."

POTION #162

"Character is activated
when life meets the dust."

POTION #163

"Knowledge and ignorance
are a spoon full of
pain... The first will
open your eyes to a bright
light, give you some well-
deserved roses, and then
introduce you to the
thorns' purposes... while
the other one... will
blind your eyes... numb
your soul, and slow you
down... The time has
come... Where will you
dine?"

POTION #164

"The greatest achievement
of all is to maintain a
rich subconscious while
the reality impoverishes,
a strong castle while the
city crumbles... a smile
while the sky cries... a
balanced moving ship,
while another Titanic
keeps sinking."

POTION #165

"Lead me to fountains that
carry your water... places
that are lit by your
love... people that know
your name... streets that
lead to a positive
change... In the end, I
can only hope to see and
understand... that my
dream and your WILL... are
spelled the same way..."

POTION #166

"Thinking is outdated...
Doing is so trendy... So
stand up..walk this
fashion show... and put on
the best smile when you
strike a pose."

POTION #167

"'Against all odds' ... I
have always enjoyed the
sound of these words...
Maybe because I believe in
miracles... Maybe because
I see beauty beyond the
given... Maybe... because
I crave to see...
something else...
something new···something···
that spells YOU!!!"

POTION #168

"Perfection is not the
root of success.

Confidence is..."

POTION #169

"The wealth starts from
deep inside... It's called
love... Love gives birth
to happiness... When she
grows up, she becomes a
natural makeup that
perfects the beauty of a
person... The beauty will
marry character. Their
life will be remarkable...
only if the last name of
the character··· spells
Solid... Pure... and
Stronger..."

POTION #170

"Sharing God with the
world... is like giving
them the secret steps to a
successful business."

POTION #171

"If you are afraid of
dogs' bark... how will you
save yourself from wolves'
anger?"

POTION #172

"Happiness is not a
destination... It's a
state of being... You
don't find it somewhere...
You uncover it from
within."

POTION #173

"Whenever you feel that an
invisible door has stopped
your dream... just
remember... devil is a
liar... There is a rainbow
behind every doubt...
There's happiness behind
every tear... There's
victory behind every hard
work... There are answers
behind every blessed
heart. Don't give up. Look
up and ask!!!"

POTION #174

"Dealing with a
nonprofessional is like
dating 'a boy'... You talk
about world change, while
he proudly recalls his
achievements in beer
games..."

POTION #175

"The only time you should
doubt and stop... is when
God says No."

POTION #176

"When reality ties your
hands... don't stop and
stare... look the other
way... plan your moves to
escape... because mind
like yours can't be
paused... and heart like
yours can't be jailed...
Fly... Child of heaven...
Fly!!!"

POTION #177

"We live in a world
surrounded by leaders that
are so corrupted they make
us justify our sins··· and
not seek light..."

POTION #178

"Coincidence is nothing...

Timing is everything."

POTION #179

"The symphony of success
is spelled out by the
balance of heart and mind.
Don't let greed ruin the
equation."

POTION #180

"The result of your hard
work won't let your
present bad choices ruin
the future potentials."

POTION #181

"Sometimes nothing
happening is better than
something bad happening.
Be patient and enjoy the
silence."

POTION #182

"The power of faith. Take
a chance. Draw rainbow in
the rain. Cry hope in the
desert of pain. Light
fireworks in the darkness
of vain. Dance until your
feet bleed love... Sing
until your voice reaches
the sky... Children of
heaven hold you in their
hands... Don't be
afraid... Give faith a
chance!"

POTION #183

"Ladies, keep your heels
and standards HIGH!!! You
got one life. No
compromise. Character
tight. No beggars advice.
Dreams that fly way up
high···. Castle rocks in the
sky."

POTION #184

"You can't understand
BEAUTY, if you haven't
Lived UGLY... Don't resent
trials. Those are the
machine refiners to bring
in life DIAMONDS..."

POTION #185

"If you can measure
happiness, you are not
happy... If you can
explain love, you don't
know it... If fear limits
your choices, you are not
ready... If there is no
altruistic reason beyond
your dream... your dream
is too small and
selfish..."

POTION #186

"You want to hear your call? Stay away from hard parties and alcohol... so you can avoid hearing the words... 'Hey honey, you're hot'... Trust me that is not the answer... or even your route to happiness. Stay away from the crowd... Plan an escape... Listen to your silence... Truth will come to you and wake up your conscience. Happy you seek... Happy you'll find... Questions you have... answers will fly... Purpose you want... Be patient on that one..."

POTION #187

"Grow in wisdom, while your

soul remains a child..."

POTION #188

"You know what's the
beauty of the ugliest
thing I have met. father's
death... the fact that no
other loss can impress me
or touch my heart...
Material loss, friends
don't talk... Bf break
ups... Who cares? If my
heart survived and stood
strong for the loss of a
bloody love... Nothing
else phases me or can
touch this heart... The
ugliest facts of your
life... sometimes they can
make you so beautiful
inside... Survive,
Conquer, Roar... Beautiful
Strong Soul..."

POTION #189

"LOST Angeles... Moral
less city... where the
definition of attraction
does not involve
intelligence... inner
beauty... strength and
character... but a spark
maintained by immoral
craziness..."

POTION #190

"Happiness is the best
paycheck I have received
from this job called
life..."

POTION #191

"Probability talk is an excuse from lazy people... Scientific explanation is for the ones that don't understand passion... Statistic memorizations are for the ones that fear achievement. Don't be any of that. 1, 2, 3 percent they remind you every day... but filter that nonsense... If the one that made history listened to the world... Today, you would have never known who they really were."

POTION #192

"Tunnel vision on my
dream. Never understood
confusion or complicated
relationships. You commit
or you are out... You
follow your dream... or
you go waste time and
party... You build or you
destroy... Grey might be a
soothing zone for some...
but 'maybe' and
'confusion' are not my
style."

POTION #193

"Life is a double headed
sword... has different
sharpness and different
goals, while one
strengthens your
character... the other
will refine your soul...
While mind gets trained to
be wise... the other re-
calls what it means to be
a child... I know this
story very well... I am
the product of this
spell."

POTION #194

"Don't give anyone the
satisfaction of pain...
Don't invest the water of
your heart for ugly
games... Don't join the
roller coaster down... Be
sound... Don't invest your
time in destruction...
Don't ask permission and
belong to malfunction···
Don't ask acceptance by
darkness... Dare to stand
strong... even if that
means... you are standing
alone."

POTION #195

"Give as if you were being
evaluated... Give as if
you were being rated...
because you are all the
same... You act right only
when your actions get a
chance of praise... You
love the light and
piedestal... but refuse to
be the same when the
audience is gone... Well
here is the truth... There
is always an audience
around you... If your eyes
don't see it... that
doesn't mean it's
missing... Give
unconditionally... Every
move of yours is eternally
weighted."

POTION #196

"I confess... I am a
workaholic... I don't care
to party... achieving
excites me... My time is
all I have... picky with
whom I share... for the
one I love... abundant
that becomes... Risking
for what I love is my
other nature... appreciate
honesty... Will give you
my world if you are
pure... will take it away
if you make me a fool... I
am a lover to the bone...
but also cold as ice when
I want. I listen to my
sixth sense... You can't
hide from that."

POTION #197

"The world of a selfish
person lacks variety...
Every day they see the
same face in the mirror of
their mind... Don't be
that... Love right... Help
left... Give to the one
who is low... Smile to the
one that sits High... Give
color to your life..."

POTION #198

"It's easy to say no. It's
easy to destroy... It's
easy to ignore... Easy
easy easy... Who cares
about it? Give me a yes!
Show me how you build...
Care... Let me see... Now,
that's appealing to me..."

POTION #199

"Happiness in our lives
starts when 'have to' gets
fired... and 'love to'
gets hired."

POTION #200

"The most attractive woman
is the one that respects
herself..."

POTION #201

"Trust and Respect... are two values I won't compromise. So when you make that mistake... Just know... there is no coming back..."

POTION #202

"Every time I get an atom
of fear... words of that
stranger ring in my
ears... Before going on
stage... Don't be nervous
or doubt... You were
chosen by Him and packed
with talent. Be confident
and proud... His light
will shine on you! And
that's what I do... I do!
It is not me... It is
always Him!"

POTION #203

"Confidence is the most beautiful machine...

Staying busy is its gasoline."

POTION #204

"The knock on heaven's door won't ever disappoint you.

So tell me why you seek pain... knocking on the earthly, broken, and molded?"

POTION #205

"Tears are body's way to
say: 'I'm not comfortable
with the pain my thoughts
are making me go
through... I need to
choose differently."

POTION #206

"Life is better without
expectations...

and happier without
perfection..."

POTION #207

"Be calm and rule the world... Be patient and move every stone... Be you... even when you don't fit the puzzle... Be authentic... beyond everything else that is rotten... Be loving... beyond every pain... Be giving... no matter who, what, and where... Don't read books of rules to success... History was made from the ones that broke those nonsense... BE YOU... and embrace one true fact... In God's eyes... You are a success."

POTION #208

"I don't want a good
lie... I want a honest
truth... Because the first
one kills me softly... But
the second one hurts me
rightly..."

POTION #209

"I am ONLY responsible of
the intentions behind what
I say and feel... not of
the way the world
perceives."

THE BOOK

POTION #210

"Breathe Love... Date
success... Marry
Happiness... Divorce pain.
Commit to nothing less
than perfect... and shout
loud... I am worth it."

POTION #211

"What I have... does not
determine who I am..."

POTION #212

"I walk... You lead... I
ask... You give... I
cry... You wipe tears... I
am happy... cause you are
near... Hold my hand and
never let go... I wanna
close my eyes... fly with
You... and never fall..."

POTION #213

"This is my love equation:
When my heart and eyes
align... and you are lit
by a heavenly light ...
then I will call you
mine."

POTION #214

"Give the world the
benefit of silence.

Don't judge. Listen. It
might surprise you."

POTION #215

"Every day I get closer to
you, every day I learn
more... you are a
challenge, a lot of work.
You demand respect... You
are the tool I need to
express myself. My heart
loves you. You give color
to my blood. I love you,
Music. Can we be partners
for life?"

POTION #216

"I have created a world
made up of people that
lift me up... If your
words are less pretty than
your silence, I will shut
you out. I have no time to
feed anybody's poison.
Here is an advice... While
I fly wrapped up with good
souls... you can take care
of that bitter seed
disease you caught on..."

POTION #217

"Bounce as if you were
walking on permanent
springs. Fly as if you
were born with beautiful
wings. Create a world
inside of the world of the
world you want to
change... Give it your
name... Live it your
way... Invite your
guests... Mind over
matter... No
corporation... No
regulation... No rules...
No machines... No
clones... Just
breathing... living being
that understand what hurts
should not be repeated...
and what is love should
not be limited..."

POTION #218

"The biggest achievement
in life is the gained
control over my mind... We
face fears... Embrace
adventure... Reject
doubts. Accept truths...
We live, love, and hope to
anchor another soul... but
we also know when to let
go. Me and my mind... Best
friends for life..."

POTION #219

"The best is not achieved
by the best,

but by the ones who don't
give loss a chance ..."

POTION #220

"You were not born with
the skills to be a great
friend, an awesome child,
a perfect mother/ father,
an amazing gf/bf, a cool
sister/brother, a one of a
kind wife/husband... It's
OK to make mistakes... to
fail... to try again...
It's OK to figure it out
as you go... For a
successful result... just
start with two steps:
forgiveness and love..."

POTION #221

"I taught myself to
believe that every closed
door or an unfulfilled
want... was not because I
wasn't good enough, but
because I was so good that
I deserved something
better... and that way of
thinking gave me a spark
of love and confidence."

POTION #222

"Attitude creates destiny. Find the key inside you⋯ that confidence that today might purr..but which is made to roar..The fruits of opportunities are ripe and ready. This is your time. Go get it!!!⋯"

POTION #223

"I don't recall everything
from past career
upbringing, but I can tell
you few things... my
training came from a
school called HEART.
Director was called
PERSISTENCE. He was a bit
strict, but I learned to
understand his reasoning.
I was bullied by FEAR and
DOUBTS, but never accepted
the VICTIM role... I
auditioned for the HERO
part and ALWAYS won... My
work was graded by my
favorite teacher. Her name
was PASSION... She was
just so beautiful and
perfect... During all
those years of work... I

THE BOOK

had a deep crush on a boy
called LOVE... I followed
him everywhere... He
taught me LIFE and
introduced me to his twin
sister... called
FORGIVENESS... I can't
complain. My life so far
has been a fairy tale."

POTION #224

"Every bad seed you choose
to carry,

becomes a bug that itches
your being..."

POTION #225

"I have a deep respect and
admiration for young and
successful people... It
shows me intelligence,
wisdom, priorities that go
deeper than the surface...
and it is just pure
attraction... I get sick
of beautiful potential
lights being a potato
couch or sinking their
soul in alcohol and
drugs... thinking they are
discovering the second
America... or maybe
changing the misery in
Africa... I want to love
the first forever... and
slap the devil out of the
second... But then I
realize... Free Will...

THE BOOK

Not everyone can hear...
Time is limited... Let's
just pray and hope...
there will be an
awakening... after all."

POTION #226

"When they are close, you
project your wishes in
what they could be, but
are not... When they are
gone, you objectively see
the truth of who they are.
Sometimes you realize you
did them wrong, Sometimes
you realize you put up
with much... Don't
regret... You can tie
their shoes but not make
their feet walk. One hand
doesn't clap alone. Make
sure, your actions, words,
and thoughts hurt no
one... and with that, your
job is done."

POTION #227

"Charm and class will get
your attention... while
intelligence and honesty
will steal your heart."

POTION #228

"You can't demand rewards
for your actions⋯
especially when it comes
to emotions... They are so
delicate and pure... They
are born... not masterly
produced... Be good...
because that's who you
are... Give... because it
makes you happy...
Sacrifice⋯ because it
fulfills you beyond the
limits... but don't demand
all the world to do the
same... They don't carry
the same DNA... Let it
Be... Take a chance... You
might get back less... or
more... who knows... the
attraction of the
unknown... Let go of
control..."

POTION #229

"Don't get occupied with
BAD too deep, if you want
GOOD to find you, and set
you free."

POTION #230

"After a long day at work,
the best produced song is
silence. Peace. Thoughts
relaxing. Soul recharges
in positivity... cuz I
know negative thinking
will only destroy me."

POTION #230

"So often we get scared of
something amazing
approaching our life... be
it a person or a career
opportunity. We are afraid
we are not worth it... or
we can't handle it...
Amazing is not for
everyone... It is true...
But if God brings it in
your life... then embrace
it... and trust⋯ you have
the ability to handle
it..."

POTION #231

"The energy your image
brings... is just an
extension of what your
soul lived and what your
heart wants."

POTION #232

"Dreaming is the vision
God gave you about your
life... If it's in your
heart... It will be in
your path."

POTION #233

"Sometimes I wonder of the
right guy falling for the
wrong girl... and the
right girl falling for the
wrong guy... and the
relationship drama people
choose... and the
challenge that they
crave... and I think of
the possible great guy and
girl... who is there...
but there is that
distortion... that missed
train··· that failed call
in between two people...
and you wonder... why? How
come?... It could have
been great... what you
think... is what you hear
today... What you don't
know is what they can

become for you tomorrow...
Wait and you understand...
Let them go... People
choose to suffer
sometimes... and not pick
the best option that comes
to their life... you know
why? Because it wasn' t
their destiny to be
blessed with you... and
God loved you enough... to
not allow that pain
destroy you... "

POTION #234

"Life without inspiration
is like a dish without
flavor."

POTION #235

"I have seen beauty...
It's called commitment."

POTION #236

"When you escape the noise
you start to notice
oneself."

POTION #237

"You speak about how
unfair the world is when
they judge you, and then
you go and become one of
them ... when you chose
wrong and hurt yourself."

POTION #238

"I pity liars. They have
mastered the knowledge of
what sounds great,
amazing, convincing, and
desirable... yet just like
a dandelion blowing in the
wind, they don't live
long enough to enjoy the
beauty of its words."

POTION #239

"Some people are
permanently pursuing a
dream and not its
achievement... when they
get closer to tangibly
touching the results...
fear of not losing the
long term commitment with
the idea of pursuing a
dream... limits their
minds to accept that they
arrived. This common
disease is called...
always moving... never
reaching... always
searching... never
finding."

POTION #240

"I reached humility when I
start believing that world
doesn't need me."

POTION #241

"The best lesson in life
is life... you won't
understand it when they
say it... you won't
comprehend it when you
hear it...

you will learn it... when
you live it."

POTION #242

"When what you want is
across the river... you
will have to capture even
the wildest horse that
comes your way. And while
that's not the way you
imagined this fairy tale
ride... you better hang
tight and learn how to
ride."

POTION #243

"Eve was created to fix Adam's problem, used to destroy Adam's blessing, and lived to nurture the existence of the same story. I'm not anymore surprised of the girl falling for the wrong man trying to 'fix' him, or the divorce and bitterness that comes after 'I do' ⋯which then continues too breed the same drama genes⋯ It's called.... 'you were born for this.'"

POTION #244

"Some people come in your
life and think they can
feed you an empty
spoon..or make you drunk
through an empty cup...
Both times you understand
the truth..but chose to
have faith that your
kindness will somehow make
them understand that you
deserve more than the
emptiness of their
tricks... Most of the
time...is like a knock on
the deaf person's door...
And there goes the
truth...You can buffer
surfaces.. but you can't
change character..."

POTION #245

"Character is the
greatest outfit I ever
wore. Heart is the most
beautiful makeup that
creates confidence and
much more. Passion is the
most amazing scent you
can't pay enough to own.
The warmth of a true soul
is an investment with no
loss."

About
Anjeza Angie Gega

Anjeza Angie Gega was born in Tirana, Albania. The Daughter of a science teacher and a mechanic father, both of whom were artistically talented but couldn't pursue it because of political control and limitations. Against all odds, relying on her passions, inherited artistic talents, and an outspoken attitude of "I will do what feels right", Anjeza Angie Gega decided to listen to her desires more than her fears.

Reading, Dancing, Singing, Studying, Acting, Creating and embracing extracurricular physical activities were the highlight of her childhood while coping with the economic status of her family. Never crying about her past nor complaining about the present, she constantly kept her eyes into the future.

Anjeza is a professional singer, actress, dancer, and author that aims to make an emotional and financial positive difference in the world. Her professional world trips, since a very early age, reinforced an early maturity and objective view of the world, which then inspired this quote book that aims to wake up some hope, strength, enlightenment, inspiration, and self-realization.

Anjeza Angie Gega holds two degrees, one in Broadcasting and another in Communication. She also studied Psychology in the affiliated UK Sheffield University located in Greece. After interning to become a part time journalist while being an artist, she realized that TV media was too politically corrupt and controlled for her to be part of it. She chose a different path, a path that will take her away from suppression of truth, into a circle where making a difference came from a genuine resource of love.

Bringing truth is strongly echoed in many of her quotes. She doesn't write to impress, but rather to identify, admit mistakes, find strength, suggest better choices, and overcome negativity by embracing light.

"I am far from perfect. I haven't conquered life. I haven't magically become permanently smart and never mistaken after bad choices. I still fall, crawl, cry, smile... but most importantly I try again... I stand up. Many of these quotes are not preaching... but alerting others and my conscience as well... Mind for some reason believes faster the information that comes from outside. So I chose to trick my mind and teach her something as an outsider" -she says about her book. She hopes her experiences and thoughts in this quote book will be perceived well by a diverse audience and they will make a difference in their life, because she lives for it.

Find more:
www.angiegega.com

www.ingramcontent.com/pod-product-compliance
Lightning Source LLC
LaVergne TN
LVHW051459080426
835509LV00017B/1833